CRIME 3.0

THE RISE OF GLOBAL CRIME IN THE XXIˢᵗ CENTURY

ALAIN BAUER

Westphalia Press
An imprint of the Policy Studies Organization

Crime 3.0:
The Rise of Global Crime in the XXIST Century

Westphalia Press
An imprint of Policy Studies Organization
1527 New Hampshire Ave., NW
Washington, D.C. 20036
dgutierrezs@ipsonet.org

ISBN-13: 978-1-935907-66-4
ISBN-10: 1935907662

Cover design by Taillefer Long at Illuminated Stories:
www.illuminatedstories.com

Updated material and comments on this edition
can be found at the Westphalia Press website:

www.westphaliapress.org

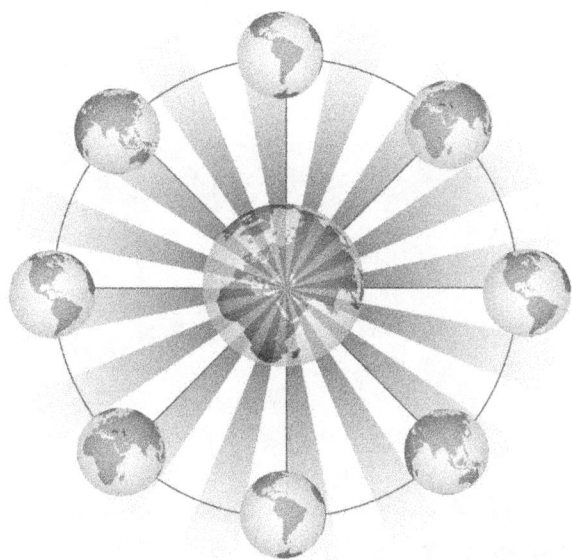

CONTENTS

FOREWORD

IT IS STILL POSSIBLE TO BE SURPRISED

As Alain Bauer says, it is still possible for crimes to surprise us. To be sure, we always enjoy the conventional crimes presented in novels and in the movies, and at times it seems that jewelry thieves have been lowered from every urban skylight, that there are no banks left without tunnels dug by enterprising robbers, and that almost anyone worth kidnapping has been held hostage.

But as Bauer points out, criminals have an adaptive genius. That is not too strong a way to put the matter. Let us give credit where credit is due. We are outfoxed all the time by new versions of thievery, not the least being the ways in which the computer can snatch money and identity. The scale of the thefts is awesome.

This of course begs the question as to how the challenges can be met, and it is one of the strengths of Bauer's arguments that his writing is founded on the principle that we need, with considerable immediacy, to press the formal study of crime in the academy and to have more resources channeled to that end. The present fragmented and incomplete situation is analogous to trying to teach medicine without teaching anatomy, or astronomy without telescopes. The approach in universities if they do deign to study the subject is often relegated to adjuncts and regarded by the more established departments with disdain.

Given the prejudices of conventional scholars towards the subject, it is no wonder that the response to crime has been inept, grows increasingly inadequate, and often means that the good guys are outclassed by the bad guys. The root servers discussed by Bauer are a good case in point. They might be likened to nuclear power plants with inadequate safeguards. Why France has in effect abdicated control in this area is a mystery, but the possible consequences will be far more unpleasant than those accompanying a cinematic quick snatch of a masterpiece from an art gallery.

We are indebted to Alain Bauer for his persistence in sounding the alarm about the situation. One only hopes that someone will hear the bell that he rings.

Paul Rich,
President,
Policy Studies Organization

CRIME 3.0

**THE RISE OF GLOBAL CRIME
IN THE XXIST CENTURY**

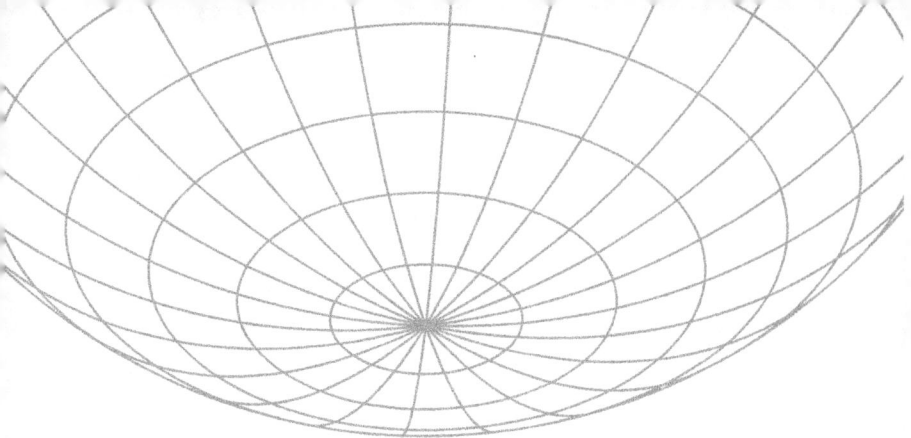

INTRODUCTION

Nowadays, we see crime, we read about crime, and we live crime in the heat of the moment, as it happens. Internet, Twitter, and the social networks have shrunk space and time. What in the past might have taken the general public a few months, a few weeks, few days or even as little as a few hours to discover now barges into our lives immediately, wherever we may be.

This rapidity does have its advantages but also one insuperable flaw: where there is no clear perspective, information loses its coherence, wiping out true understanding. A piece of information, rarely verified, and a few denials are generally the only elements we have to maintain some semblance of balance. Everyone wants to move faster, with greater impact and, above all, at whatever cost, ensure uninterrupted output.

The commentary commentators drown out the few, often cautious experts, called on to give weight to a report, but keen to have a clear picture before speaking out. They make sweeping assertions while seeming to question, recount their own truths while seeming to inform and muddy the waters while seeming to clarify.

No subject is spared but crimes and terrorism seem favorites, with their sensational side and the media world's appetite for events that can fill a special edition.

Much ink has been spilled over the origins of organized crime and how it has changed (the "latest godfather," as the headline often reads, is all too soon replaced by a successor), developments in terrorism (many "lone wolves" have been uncovered even when they act together and travel abroad to training camps) and any crime event considered exceptional or unprecedented. At the same time, little or nothing is said about major changes in what we might call the "dark side of globalization."

In recent years, with colleagues and friends, we have been trying to attract public attention to these phenomena, which are a key factor at the heart of the great financial "crashes" of world history, which are so seldom given their true weight. They are less spectacular than vendettas, killings or hostage takings and their impact on the lives of individuals and countries largely exceeds what our vision of them dictates.

Global crime, escalating from an individual or gang to a "criminal enterprise" developing its local activity through a multitude of international contacts, is rooted in the first globalization phase of the end of the nineteenth century. It is therefore essential to analyze current developments as a logical continuity to avoid confusing what is new with what we have simply forgotten.

Given the sweeping changes now occurring in criminal behavior, it is even more vital for us to move away from conservative routine. Above all, we need to sidestep being overrun yet again by a new reality, preparing for a war that has already been lost in an earlier phase.

We are clearly at war: a territorial war; entire regions in many countries are controlled by organized criminals banded together into veritable armies; a war against financial crime that sustains and exacerbates "official" economic crises and may even be their direct cause; a cyber-war in which the classic confrontations between countries and companies are extended onto a digital front and intertwine dangerously with strict-sense criminal activities.

These are new wars with new warriors: on the fertile ground of religious fanaticism, homegrown terrorism competes with exported terrorism; emerging hybrid groups are penning a new chapter in gangster terrorism; a "Lumpen-terrorism" of the dispossessed is increasingly visible. We cannot apply conventional reasoning and practices in identifying so many of these new realities, which it is impossible to express in a tweet, the new reference for our modern "thought."

Criminal wars, financial crises fueled by crime, terrorism, and cyber-crime: the topics broached may seem varied but under the surface, they are the same, part of the multi-faceted world of the illegal in all its richness and breadth: a world of villains, thugs, fraudsters, swindlers, fanatics, and assassins; a world contemplated and studied here in its emerging form; a world of lasting peril which, more than ever, should fire up the imagination of the people and provoke measured, proactive and effective policies from governments.

Yet in France, we are hampered by an unfortunate time lag: how, with seventeenth century moral values, an eighteenth century penal code, a nineteenth century policing structure, and twentieth century equipment, can we combat twenty-first century criminality?

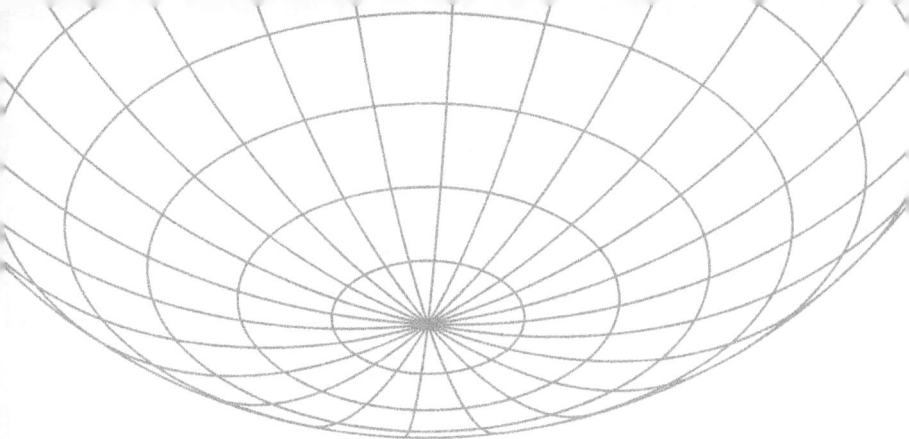

EMERGING GLOBAL CRIMINALITY

"Latest crime news," we say, but how do we know whether this news is relevant? Are the phenomena discussed here the right ones? Are we looking at the truth or are we victims of media mirages or "false positives"? Could we be mixing up the alarm with the background noise?

Let us open up another perspective. We will climb (conceptually) the mountain and, from its summit, look ahead along the road. Philosophy lets us do this. We need to "take a step backwards," like in an art gallery, to admire a canvas, to see it from a distance.

To conceptualize twenty-first century crime, we need to start by setting it in a wider framework, a longer time perspective. Crime has considerable historic depth. The phenomenon is anything but new and not just a matter for large cities or national governments. Identity theft, illegal immigration, drug trafficking, terrorist attacks, human trafficking, and financial crime are developing between continents and hemispheres. Yet, there is too often a tendency to overestimate just how new these world problems are. Without a historic perspective, it is difficult to judge how the problems are changing.

The generation living just before World War I was the first to have to tackle crime on an international scale. Towards the end of the nineteenth century, governments, commentators, and opinion-makers had begun to ponder the shrinking world ushered in by technologies and their cultural, social, and economic impact on criminal behavior. They noticed that alarming changes in ordinary criminal behavior were occurring, alongside the emergence of new forms of crime, such as anarchism, white slavery, and imported criminality. A new breed of experts that went by the name criminologists used the language of science in attempt to obtain a planetary vision of the phenomenon.

INITIAL GLOBALIZATION OF CRIME

In a remarkable, little book that passed largely unnoticed, the English Professor, Paul Knepper, describes the emergence of international crime[1] in imperial Great Britain in the years between 1881 and 1914. He explores how the international dimension is the only practical way of understanding crime in Great Britain in this period and beyond. To do so, we need to look back over the progress made in transport, communication, and trade relations, resulting in an interconnected world. This is

---

1   The Invention of International Crime - A Global Issue in the Making (1881–1914). Palgrave.

the era in which police officers, journalists, novelists, and other commentators described the rise in professional criminals, international fraudsters, who used the new technologies of the age against their victims.

However, this internationalization was not purely technology-based. It also had an imperial dimension. This means that the conditions in which the political authorities of the British Empire encouraged this international-scale crime decoding work needs to be kept in mind. As a result of this, the Colonial Service turned to analogies to comprehend individuals and communities that could not be understood according to conventional patterns of thought. The "colonial" investigations resulted in comparisons between domestic criminality and the sense of a "globalized criminal class."

FEAR OF INTERNATIONAL CONSPIRACY

The process should be completed by research into migrations. In response to a wave of Anti-Semitism following the assassination of Czar Alexander II in 1881, millions of Jews fled to the West. This huge migration fostered foreign criminality, persecuting the persecuted, surfing the wave, and profiting from or revealing true self through it. Anti-Semites raised the specter of this type of criminal behavior and stirred up fear of a population imported from within the protective borders of the Russian Empire. This led to the passing of the Aliens Act, the first legal attempt to control immigration in Great Britain and the first step towards an international policy seeking to establish identities by making passports and identity papers obligatory. The fear of foreign crime was based not only on the poverty of these communities and where they came from but on an alleged international conspiracy...

They were suspected of controlling a large portion of the "white slavery" market and trafficking in women and girls for prostitution. In fact, Jewish philanthropists invested a great deal of money in the fight against this scourge. One measure was the creation of a Jewish Association for the Protection of Women and Girls. This problem quickly attracted international attention and prompted a coordinated international response. The National Vigilance Association, founded in 1885, organized the first international conference to discuss the problem which resulted in the signature of the first international treaty on the subject in 1904. Supporters of this legal framework saw immigration, accelerated by steam ship travel, as the principle source of this scourge, coupled with the market in "artists" and the new acceptance of women moving around alone in the modern world.

THE FIRST "LONDONISTAN"?

The assassination of the Czar in 1881 also marked the beginning of a new type of criminal behavior: the anarchist attack. In the early 1880s, anarchists or those who claimed to follow this political movement began to launch bomb attack campaigns in Europe and North America, murdering half a dozen heads of State, including U.S. President William McKinley in 1901. London became an anarchist refuge and the era was marked by the tension produced by their presence. We could call it the first "Londonistan... A first foiled attack was recorded in 1894 when a French anarchist was killed as he tried to destroy the Greenwich Observatory. The International Anti-Anarchy Defense Conference held in Rome in 1898 to respond to these threats ended without a final agreement being reached.

FOR THE RECORD: CHICAGO AND MARSEILLE, TEXTBOOK CASES

At the end of the nineteenth century, in a developing trade in white women and other forms of international trafficking, Marseille, located at the heart of trade routes between Africa, Europe, America, and Asia, was ideally situated as a center for criminal forms of trade. The authorities became concerned about hired thugs with their tightening grip on the city. The sharp rise in drug trafficking tipped the balance: in the 1920s, this highly structured underworld, headed by gang bosses and their enforcers or henchmen, and governed by its traditions (the law of silence), prospered with the help of rampant police force corruption, close ties between criminals and local politicians, an, above all, a boom in alcohol and drug trafficking. Marseille became the nerve center of the trade between North America (an important growth area for consumption) and Asia (for production). Although, for a long time, the leading Western countries and Japan took on a role of "lawful dealers," waging an opium war to reestablish the drug trade in China despite it having recently been outlawed there (between 1839 and 1842, then 1856 and 1860), changing attitudes were fueling a trend towards prohibition

9

almost everywhere and led to the signature, in January 1912, of the first international drug control treaty, the Hague International Opium Convention.

In 1925, the "Marseille Godfathers," Paul Carbone and François Spirito (one Italian, the other Corsican), held a meeting in Egypt. They formed a prostitution, trafficking, racketeering, and extortion partnership and invented the first case of criminal activity "industrialization" in the West. The first factories producing heroin from opium imported raw from Indochina, and later Turkey (processed in France and distributed in the U.S.) were established in Marseille in 1937. In Chicago, Alfonse Capone took full advantage of the perverse effects of Prohibition, investing in the bootlegging of black market alcohol and industrial-scale money laundering. Following the purest rules of an advanced free-market economy, they set up business on the shores of the Mediterranean and on the other side of the Atlantic, practiced vertical and horizontal integration, invested in research and development, developed staff incentives, extended their trade areas, and engaged in tax planning. Their treatment of their competitors seems to be the only facet of their business that was a great deal more "final" than in honest sectors of the economy.

At the time of the French Liberation, their successors, the Guérini brothers, who were more successful in their choice of political allies during the Occupation, made new alliances, extending their empire and diversifying their businesses, investing in cigarette smuggling to supplement their international narcotics trade, swelled by their close relationship with the New York Godfather,

Lucky Luciano. The French Connection was born. The first international trading agreement for the distribution of industrially produced heroin was made in the 1960s.

In Marseille, it took the Liberation to end the Carbone and Spirito Empire. It was taken over by the Guérini Brothers whose political alliances had been more astute. In Chicago, Elliott Ness, a Prohibition Bureau agent, put an end to Capone's career with charges of tax evasion. Franck Nitti, then Tony Accardo, took over operations without great difficulty, but with less provocation and lower visibility.

The Guérini Brothers lost their stranglehold over Marseille at the beginning of the 1960s, after their attempt, with others, to extend their hold over Parisian gaming circles. The result was the "gambling war" of the mid-1960s, resulting in Antoine's murder and Barthélémy's imprisonment. A new figure, Gaëtan Zampa, then came onto the scene. Marseille became the setting for a bloody gang war. In 1973, Zampa's ambitions clashed with the aspirations of Francis Vanverberghe, or "Francis Le Belge," who was deeply involved in narcotics trafficking. The conflict resulted in bloody street battles resulting in many deaths but creating the heyday of the "scandal papers" until Zampa's arrest and imprisonment in November 1983.

The first decade of this century was particularly dark for the Marseille underworld. On September 27, 2000, Francis Le Belge, who had taken the Marseille Mafia in hand despite living in Paris, was murdered. Two years after his death, the Marseille criminal scene burst into violence in a merciless war between gypsy criminals, for a time led by Farid Berrahma, the *Rôtisseur*, Corsicans from Bastia, and homegrown criminals from Marseille. The increasing competition between rival gangs led to revenge murders and reckonings but they were also fueled by the ever-younger protagonists involved in these routs, who lacked the professionalism, cool composure, and code of conducts of the old Mafia Godfathers.

Since then, the blows inflicted by the police to a number of gangs (arrest of the Campanella Brothers and Bernard Barresi in 2010, imprisonment of Jacques Cassandri in January 2011) have helped to open the way to other groups from the housing projects. They are waging outright war to safeguard their territory and protect their business interests.

A war of succession and a war of secession are being waged simultaneously, which, with the accidental death of Jean Gé Colonna, the last gangland peace mediator, has resulted in the fragmentation of the local criminal territory.

There have been similar developments in the U.S. with the arrival of powerful criminal gangs from Latin America, including Mexico and Guatemala. As is often the case, there is evidence of a "postcolonial" effect on changes to the criminal environment.

Therefore, without us realizing it, globalization and crime have progressed together, at first in parallel and later through direct cross-connections, with each fueling the other. The era of international criminal behavior is now in full flow.

Unfortunately, in criminal matters, like terrorism, which is just another facet of crime, the new is too often just the forgotten.

Yet, it is still possible to be surprised. Controlling territories, conquering other spaces, attracting attention through bullying and bragging, provoking governments like Capone or Escobar, creating strategies of fear through the murders of General Della Chiesa or judges Borsellino and Falcone, before adopting a lower profile, criminal organizations, especially in the financial sector, have learned how to be forgotten.

However, more recently, some have taken another path of "freeing up" entire regions to create "Narco-States." On an entirely different scale to petty score-settling, there is a higher level of conflict mobilizing veritable armies: criminal warfare.

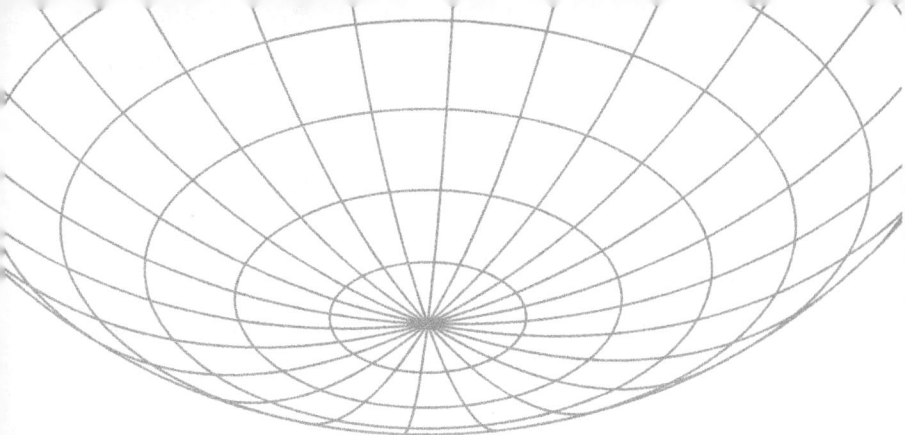

AGE OF CRIMINAL WARFARE

For a long time, criminals were seen as curious individuals, sometimes backed by a small group (a gang, crew, or posse) who forged a myth or legend over a more or less spectacular career. Gang chiefs, serial killers, or mass murderers built their image at the pace of the developing means of communication.

What medium could survive without its crime pages? Yet, out of the limelight, criminal empires control entire regions and have hijacked their place at the table of world geopolitics.

The public, journalists, and sometimes even the police have developed a fascination for these "lovable rogues" and the road movies depicting a romanticized version of facts condensed in space and time.

Edgar Hoover's reluctant acknowledgement of Mafia presence in the U.S. following the "Apalachin Raid" at the end of 1957[2] marked final recognition of the phenomenon of organized crime. For a long time, it could only be identified through the heads of families operating "business models" involving largely underestimated conventional criminal activities (racketeering, prostitution, and trafficking). Organized crime has moved on a great deal since then.

AN IMPRESSIVE GEOPOLITICAL SPACE

Criminal globalization has not only outstripped the globalization of individual countries, it has pierced the heart of such countries. Criminal cartels have exploited the weakness of some countries to establish territories no longer restricted to a few pockets of largely-impenetrable jungle like the FARC in Colombia or the Burmese Golden Triangle.

Since the 1990s, the Maras (or *Marabuntas*, an army of legionary ants destroying everything in their path) have been multiplying and gaining ground in El Salvador, Honduras, and Guatemala. They are also progressively moving south into Panama, Costa Rica, and Nicaragua. They can be found in Brazil, Mexico, and Colombia. According to Xavier Raufer[3], there are

---

2   A conference of North American gangland bosses was organized in Apalachin (New York State) at the home of mobster Joseph Barbara in November 1957. A hundred or so Mafia "capos" from all over the United States, Canada, and Italy attended this meeting. Sharp-eyed local law enforcement officers, intrigued by the arrival of a mass of luxury limousines in a small village, planned a police raid to establish the identity of those present, prompting some of those in attendance to flee into the nearby woodland. Until then, Edgar Hoover, head of the FBI, had refused to acknowledge the existence of organized crime in the United States.

3   *Géopolitique de la Mondialisation Criminelle* (The Geopolitics of Criminal Globalization)—PUF, 2013.

more than 7,000 members of these criminal organizations, involved in a wide-range of criminal activities, in established international relationships with entrenched Mafia groups in Italy and the U.S. The Maras have a marked foothold in California (18th Street Gang or *Mara Dieciocho*). They appear to have struck up agreements with the Mexican Zetas.

The cost to countries in the region is considerable. According to the World Bank, criminal activity is the root-cause of almost 8% in lost gross domestic product (GDP) and is a serious threat to development.

In Mexico, it is said that the narcotics industry directly employs 450,000 people, with a concentration in the north of the country. Twenty-three of the country's thirty-two federated states are now virtual "Narco-Republics," corrupted and infiltrated by criminals. Baja California, Chihuahua, Durango, Guerrero, Michoacán, Nuevo Leon, Sinaloa, Sonora, and Tamaulipas are the worst affected areas. Organized crime exerts "an influence" over 6% of the country's 2,438 municipalities.

In 2010, for the first time in world history, Los Zetas, a paramilitary group involved in a multitude of criminal activities, a mega-gang formed and run by deserters from the Mexican army and police force, "freed up" territory in northern Mexico on the border with the U.S. This area has since remained under its control. Any Mexican or American armed forces serviceman or civil servant straying into this area is murdered as soon as he is spotted.

Los Zetas is the name given to the criminal army formed around 15 years ago by deserters from the Mexican Special Forces recruited by the Gulf Cartel (now numbering more than 4,000 armed men sometimes operating in uniform). It now controls the majority of an area of the Rio Grande between Acuna and the major port of Matamoros.

In 2012, Los Zetas were spread over almost the whole of Mexico and Central America, from the Texan border to the Panama Canal.

However, Los Zetas are not the only criminal force to have achieved paramilitary strength. Elsewhere in Mexico, the Michoacán Cartel *Caballeros Templarios* (Knights Templar) now have the "military" capacity to mount simultaneous and coordinated attacks (with grenades and automatic weapons) against police stations, which it does regularly.

The State of Chihuahua and its capital, Ciudad Juarez (with its 1.3 million inhabitants) now form the epicenter of this criminal warfare. It forms a highly strategic drugs "corridor" (*La Linea* in Spanish) to the U.S. In two years of fierce fighting (from 2008 to 2010), the Sinaloa Cartel ousted the Juarez Cartel. During that time, recorded homicides rose by 20%. From the end of 2006 to March 2010, there were 5,000 killings. In Juarez, the murder rate rose to 165 per 100,000, compared to an average in the European Union of 2 per 100,000.

For years, Mexican cartel infighting in the north of the country has led to massacres which, in body count, have now exceeded levels recorded in the Afghan and Iraqi conflicts combined. In some Mexican towns, full-blown armies, well-equipped and in uniform, fight to take over whole communities in pitched battles. Even U.S. border patrols sometimes have to confront the armored vehicles of the cartels.

In Karachi, a city of at least 20 million people, the war continues on a daily basis between the Pashtun Taliban of the TTP (Tehrik-i-Taliban Pakistan, also more exotically called the "Anti-Criminal Activity Committee"), the remains of the Bhutto dynasty's PPP (Pakistani People's Party), and the MQM (Mohajir Qaumi Movement), in operations largely in excess of those ordered by the Taliban against Pakistan and the West.

Piracy was increasing at an almost exponential rate in the Gulf of Aden and along the Somali coast, dominating an ever-wider area of the ocean, until a robust international mobilization achieved a progressive reduction in activity.

The often-discrete Chinese authorities publicly announced their success in dismantling deeply-entrenched triads and the arrest of thousands of individuals for their criminal activities.

Organized criminal actions have become outright military operations. Gangs have increasingly modern resources at their disposal. They are capable of resisting the most structured of forces and not only in debilitated States.

It is still difficult for some major countries to admit that the world around them is in chaos, despite their efforts. Government agencies still dream of a bygone world where superpowers alone can impose a higher order, disrupted only by a few criminals content with whatever may come their way. There is always time to create a media concept for dealing with "hyper-criminality" to follow on from "hyper-terrorism." Yet, crime is on the rise while we wait for this late revelation. It is now a major influence in finance and is forging itself an impressive geopolitical space.

Above all, it is acquiring increased and more effective control over access to our "lifeblood" because money, especially electronic money, cannot sidestep network crime which, little by little, is taking hold of legitimate finance and the lawful economy so that we can now legitimately talk of "criminal finance."

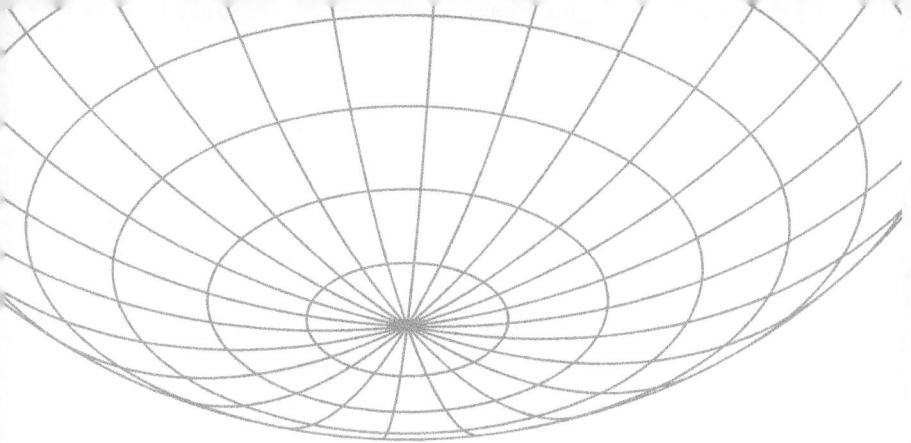

CRIMINAL FINANCIAL CRISES

Starting with the "Yakuza Recession" of the 1980s, then the U.S. Savings and Loans Crisis of the same era, followed by Mexico, Russia, and Thailand, a series of financial crises with a more-or-less marked criminal dimension has rocked the world's leading countries over the last 30 years. Central regulators paid no attention to this phenomenon despite International Monetary Fund (IMF) estimates of a quantity of dirty cash of between 1% and 5% of world GDP. The world of crime has become a financier of primary importance.

THE SAVINGS AND LOANS HOLD UP

The Savings and Loans Crisis devastated U.S. savings associations in the 1980s. Almost two-thirds of these institutions went out of business through bankruptcies that were clearly fraudulent. The crisis is estimated to have cost around 160 billion USD, 124.6 billion of which was doled out by the U.S. Treasury, a cost equivalent to World War II[4].

Jean-François Gayraud reminds us that, according to the U.S. General Accounting Office (the federal accounts auditing body) and to the numerous judicial, university, and journalistic investigations conducted since, these bankruptcies resulted from massive and systematic misappropriations carried out from inside the savings associations themselves by senior executives (white collar crime), sometimes in association with members of traditional gangland groups.

Effective governance of these "thrift" associations had become lax. The Garn-St. Germain Depository Institutions Act of 1982 had deregulated the sector regardless of its particular sensitivity to criminal ambitions. Local Mafias leapt into the breach. Based on falsified documents, an increasing number of loans at very low interest rates were granted to "friends" on very "flexible" terms and conditions. At the same time, a systematic use of "creative" accounting concealed the colossal losses. In 1987, the U.S. Attorney General acknowledged massive frauds.

---

4   On this crisis see (in French) Jean-François Gayraud "*Crises Financières: la Dimension Criminelle*" (Financial Crises, the Criminal Dimension), *Défense Nationale et Sécurité Collective*, December 2008; Jean-François Gayraud "*La Dimension Criminelle de la Crise des Subprimes*" (The Criminal Dimension in the Subprime Crisis), *Diplomatie*, Special Edition No. 8, April-May 2009 and (in English) Kitty Calavita, Henry N. Pontell, and Robert H. Tillman, "*Big Money Crime, Fraud and Politics in the Savings and Loan Crisis*" (University California Press, 1997).

The vast majority of the ill-gotten gains raked in by the fraudsters were secreted away into tax havens. It also led to the collapse of the U.S. construction market, which fell from 1.8 million new homes per year to only 1 million between 1986 and 1991.

THE YAKUZA RECESSION[5]

The Japanese Yakuza are some of the most powerful organized crime organizations. In 2008, there were nearly 90,000 members amalgamated into three leading criminal federations (Inagawa Kai, Yamaguchi Gumi, and Sumiyoshi Rengo). These organizations are involved in the usual array of crimes: racketeering and protection, arms trafficking, prostitution, pornography, illegal gaming (Pachinko), and merchandise smuggling.

During the 1980s, the "Jusen" (real estate lending cooperatives) were frequent victims of falsified loans, many of which were applied for by companies "reeking" of Yakuza involvement. According to the Japanese government, in 1999 alone, more than 4% of loans to finance construction found themselves in the hands of organized crime syndicates. In 2002, it was estimated that there were still "bad loans" (Mafia loans, for the most part) valued between 800 and 1,600 billion USD. According to Japan's national police force, around half of these "bad loans" were non-recoverable as they were held by

---

5   On this crisis see Jean-François Gayraud, *"Le Monde des Mafias, Géopolitique du Crime Organisé"* (The Mafia World, Geopolitics of Organized Crime) Odile Jacob, 2005 and 2008; Jean-François Gayraud, *Crises Financières: la Dimension Criminelle* (Financial Crises, the Criminal Dimension), *Défense Nationale et Sécurité Collective*, December 2008.

organized crime. Goldman Sachs confirmed the estimate in relation to business loans. According to the T channel, NHK, two in five Japanese companies had Yakuza links. After inflating the market, the Yakuza bought up real estate assets at slashed prices and forcibly blocked settlement of the liabilities of some companies. The rare bankers who dared to intervene were threatened and, in some cases, murdered.

The extraordinary duration of the Japanese financial crisis, despite the many and far-reaching recovery measures, can only be understood if the criminal dimension is included in the equation. The Yakuza caused companies to absorb losses from the unpaid loans and then privatized Mafia profits. The country has still not recovered.

THE FALL OF THE RUSSIAN HOUSE[6]

The transition to a market economy in the Russian Federation began at the end of 1991. In 1992, Russia launched a massive privatization program. "Shock therapy" began in 1994 with 5% of the public sector organizations (i.e. more than 100,000 State enterprises) being privatized. This fast-paced deregulation of the economy was conducted in highly questionable circumstances.

The privatizations and control over raw materials for the most part benefitted businessmen with close connections to the Leadership. The country witnessed a grabbing of public assets, monopolized by a group of cronies. These new "robber barons" acquired notoriety and became

---

6   On this transition see Joseph Stiglitz, "*Quand le Capitalisme Perd la Tête*" (When Capitalism Loses its Head), Fayard, 2003; Joseph Stiglitz, *La Grande Désillusion* (Globalization and its Discontents), Fayard, 2002.

known as the "oligarchs." These profiteers, sometimes backed by a criminal underworld in full revival, realized that their situation was precarious and invested their ill-gotten gains abroad in tax and banking havens.

Through these "hasty" privatizations, the transition initially caused the GDP to halve. Unemployment, at a rate of less than 0.1% of the working population at the start of the 1990s, rose to 7.5% in 1994. At the same time, according to *The Lancet* (2009), the mortality rate increased four times faster in Russia than in other benchmark countries.

The economic depression culminated in the financial crisis of 1998, marked by sharp devaluation in the Ruble and a sovereign debt default. The flight of capital via criminal activity during this period is estimated at 100 billion USD.

A large portion of the funds injected into the country's economy by international institutions such as the IMF and World Bank to save it from the damaging effects of the "shock therapy" was diverted and placed outside Russia.

THE "TEQUILA CRISIS"

The 1994-95 Mexican financial crisis, known as the "Tequila Effect" was, more than anything, a "Cocaine Effect." Mexican traffickers acquired a very large share in the revenues from Columbian drugs exported to the U.S. at the beginning of the 1990s, earning themselves more than 10 billion USD per year. The business privatizations under the Salinas presidency (1988-94) provided an opportunity for "recycling" the profits from narcotics through a banking sector that had itself been privatized. Following the 1994-95 crisis, the banks owed more than 180 billion USD, for which the State Treasury was forced to assume liability

Combined with an influx of international capital, this money laundering contributed to a massive injection of enormous sums of cash into the economy and the creation of a double real estate and stock market "bubble." Although they represented only 1% to 3% of Mexican GDP in the beginning, both in trade and in banking, the narcotics dollars distorted markets in favor of Mafia networks. The "money laundering premium" earned by the drugs barons made them more competitive and able to «absorb» their competitors and yet still focus on short-term speculative investments. Access to credit enabled them to recycle dirty capital and to increase the power of its impact. The injection of narcotics dollars weakened trade and precipitated payment defaults, causing the Peso to be devalued and bringing on the financial crisis. It cost the Mexican Treasury more than 100 billion USD and increased unemployment threefold.

THE THAI BUBBLE

The 1997 Asian Crisis started in Thailand, where the scenario was a similar one. The equivalent of 1 % of Thai GDP was controlled by organized crime networks which earned their income for the most part from illegal gaming, prostitution, and trafficking in drugs exported from Burma. As in Mexico, the influx of short-term foreign capital accelerated a speculative trend. The deterioration in external accounts, made worse by the increase in the value of the U.S. Dollar and shrinkage of expert opportunities, precipitated the devaluation of the Baht.

However, the local political and financial system also played a role by massively encouraging the laundering of illegal and Mafia earnings. At the end of 1999, despite a 10% fall in Thai GDP in 1998 and real estate overcapacity in Bangkok estimated at more than three hundred thousand units, sales prices held their ground. The reason for this stability, impossible to comprehend in market terms, becomes clear if we consider the money laundering circuit impact.

THE SUBPRIME TSUNAMI[7]

As highlighted by the expert, Noël Pons[8], the mechanics of the crisis that broke out in 2009 were almost identical to that of the 1980s. Only the parties involved were different. In this new format, the banks were fed with applications for loans by mortgage brokers who made lavish promises. A number of applications were discreetly categorized as "non-documented." They were in fact faked, involving acts of fraud, scamming, abuse of trust, and forgery. Operating with the backing of

---

7   On this crisis see a number of articles by Jean-François Gayraud: "*La Dimension Criminelle de la Crise des Subprimes* (The Criminal Dimension of the Subprime Crisis), *Diplomatie*, Special Edition No. 8, April–May 2009; "*Crises Financières: la Dimension Criminelle Un An Après*" (Financial Crises, the Criminal Dimension One year On), *Défense Nationale et Sécurité Collective*, December 2009; "*Capitalisme Criminel: Subprimes ou Subcrimes?*" (Criminal Capitalism: Subprime or Subcrime?), *Cité*, No. 41, PUF, March 2010.

8   See Noël Pons, "*La Crise des Subprimes: une Aubaine pour les Criminalités?*" (Subprime Crisis: A Bonanza for Criminals) Cahiers de la Sécurité, No. 7, January–March 2009.

mortgage lenders, the brokers dispensed questionable loans, using predatory lending techniques, consisting of lending to people from vulnerable demographic groups (poor people, ethnic minorities, etc.). Credit frequently exceeded 125% of the value of the home purchased with the loan. Home values were also significantly inflated. Loans were frequently made to borrowers unable to meet capital repayments on an interest only basis, a system thriving only in conditions of speculation. The illusion persists as long as the market is still rising. The entire economy, steeped in debt, became a "pyramid economy," a gigantic Ponzi scheme.

In an attempt to conceal what was really happening, the banks tried amalgamating loans into common pools by "securitizing" them and then, in a second stage, mixing the "junk" securities with others in global structures, themselves overvalued, to produce a cocktail of fund derivatives based on nothing, but still highly speculative. Naturally, accounts were also falsified or externalized. In the third stage, the "globalized" structures were insured and then reinsured and finally sold to "investors," many of whom were domiciled in tax havens. These on-sold "receivables" were then used as leverage to raise loans from the major commercial banks that placed these "virtual securities" with other, notably foreign banks, local authorities, associations, etc. From the bottom of the ladder upwards, these dealings may not always have been blatantly fraudulent but were at least often very shady.

A few months before the outbreak of the subprime crisis, although nothing could be done to prevent it,

Michael Mukasey, Attorney General in the George W. Bush administration, curiously denounced the criminalization of the economic and financial markets on April 23, 2008, at a conference on organized crime at the Center for Strategic and International Studies (CSIS).

More recently in Europe, there was the case of the carbon VAT scam which involved buying rights to pollute, exclusive of VAT, in one European country through a dummy or shell company, with almost immediate resale on the French, English, or Italian markets, inclusive of VAT. The fraudsters pocket the VAT rate differential and disperse it between offshore accounts.

These transactions involve the fraudsters themselves, their protectors, and financiers, especially the "launderers" of the monies earned from trafficking, including in narcotics. A judge was reported in the newspaper *Le Parisien* as saying: "there is a veritable Mafia behind the carbon emissions tax and a Mafia does not hesitate to kill."

In January 2009, Serge Lepage, son of a well-known underground figure, was shot down in front of his home. It was suspected that he had been called upon as a provider of funding for carbon emission tax fraudsters.

Amar Azzoug was executed on April 30, 2010, in a brasserie in Saint-Mandé. A known former bank robber, this 35-year-old man had been implicated in carbon tax fraud and its embezzled millions. He had known that he was a marked man and had alerted the police, incriminating Samy Souied as the probable person behind the threats.

Five months later, Samy Souied himself was shot down by two men in front of the Palais des Congrès at Porte Maillot in Paris. He had just landed from Te Aviv and was due to leave again that same evening. He was carrying €30,000 in cash. The last man who had spoken to him was the former son-in-law of Claude Dray, a hugely-wealthy businessman and art collector, murdered at his mansion house in Neuilly-sur-Seine on the night of October 24/25, 2011.

There was nothing that seemingly connected this murder with the previous ones. However, his assassination does raise questions: his safe was full of jewels and other valuables but nothing was stolen

The real gangland bosses are concealed behind these "white collar" swindlers and fraudsters. These men do not forgive errors or oversights. Similarly, the "lovable rogues" of old were not inclined to forgive, and the amounts of money at stake explain this epidemic of old-fashioned 7.65 mm weapon murders.

At the beginning of February 2012, the French Court of Auditors covered this affair in its annual report. It stated:

> [...] the carbon emission quota VAT fraud is the largest tax fraud ever recorded in France in so short a time. It demonstrates failings in regulating a market in which naivety about how resourceful fraudsters can be combines with risk perception errors on the part of market administrators and government. It also highlights the inadequacy in forward planning to provide effective regulation tools for markets in which, given their characteristics, the fraud potential has been overlooked.

The Court of Auditors assessed the tax loss to the French autumn 2008 to June 2009 budget at €1.6

billion. Europol estimated the total loss within the European Union at €5 billion. Twenty or so prosecutions have now been brought involving more than a hundred individuals.

"Neither the European Commission nor Member States have shown any concern for safeguarding the conditions in which the VAT is collected," stated the Court, which underscored "the original flaws and loopholes in the system: almost unrestricted access by any natural person or corporate entity to national quota registers and the lack of external regulation." It also criticized the:

> [...] inadequate vigilance on the part of the market administrator, too superficial an applicant identity checking process, unconvincing application of duties of vigilance, market operators perceived the systemic magnitude of the fraud too late, errors and mismanagement on the part of finance ministries.

On the subject of TRACFIN, the French financial intelligence unit, the Court of Auditors noted "data processing delays incompatible with swift action to stop fraud." It also criticized the General Directorate for Public Finance for failing to "anticipate" the magnitude of the fraud, stressing that "its standard procedures were not fit for purpose" and "there was inadequate coordination between its different services."

Despite acknowledging the May 2009 decision by the Finance Ministry to alter the VAT collection method on CO2 quota transactions to stem Treasury losses, the Court of Auditors reiterated the point that there were still "persistent problems, especially of poor" or inadequate control of access to registers.

In short, as usual, the commission of enquiry only exposed what had been known for a long time (the first frauds of this type date back to the 1970s): slow-moving and cumbersome regulatory authority action; existing systems incapable of taking the criminal dimension into account.

Criminal organizations started on a small-scale to test the market, just a few hundred thousand francs to begin with. Yet, they have managed to steal several billion euros with 40 years of practical experience, like the Ponzi schemes that will soon celebrate a century of existence, and which still seem as effective as ever. What will the next stage be?

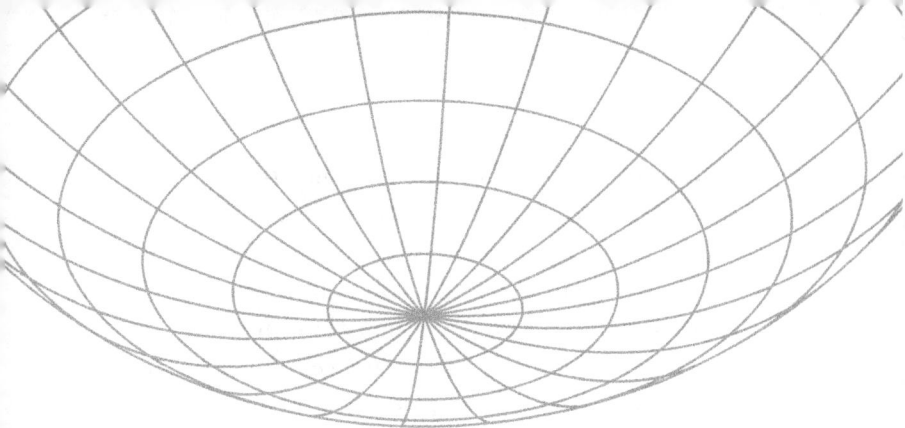

TERRORISM OR TERRORISMS?

The definition of terrorism has always been flawed. It is the largest international organizations that have the greatest difficulty in defining what terrorism is. Everyone is always someone else's terrorist or resistance fighter. This confusion in terms engenders a treatment problem: how can we cure what we cannot diagnose?

Since the reappearance, after the fall of the Berlin Wall in 1989, of a form of terrorism different to previous ones (independent of the great empires that could permit or prevent action by controlling training camps, false papers, money, weapons, and explosives), we now need to reflect carefully on the nature of homegrown or home-based terrorists who have gradually been replacing the imported kind.

The organizers of the 9/11 tragedy for the most part used agents sent into the West. Since then, the number of operatives born in the West or resident there since childhood, some of whom are converts, has increased dramatically. Although many continue to travel to other countries where preachers act as spiritual sanctioners to strengthen their criminal resolve, an increasing number of others are connected via their computers and have no need to travel, reducing their chances of being identified.

The situation is hardly new but there seems to be no limit to the capacity of the antiterrorism forces to forget the lessons of the past. The security services are still too impervious to events in the build-up to a tragedy and then need to readjust too abruptly, jumping from extreme denial to the opposite extreme.

With the case of Khaled Khelkal in 1995 and then the Roubaix Gang in 1996, France suffered the painful experience of "hybrids": half gangster, half terrorist. These half-breeds slip into the gaps between the two accepted groups, escaping the attention of security services that are unable to make the connection and to see beyond their own compartmentalization. Sixteen years later, Mohammed Merah said that things were still the same today. The matter was discussed at length in a study produced by Mitch Silber, that I supervised, for NYPD on "Radicalization in the West, the Homegrown Threat" (2006):

> [...] while the threat from overseas remains, many of the terrorist attacks or thwarted plots against cities in Europe, Canada, Australia and the U.S. have been conceptualized and planned by local residents/ citizens who sought to attack their country of residence. The majority of these individuals began as "unremarkable" – they had "unremarkable" motivations, lived "unremarkable" lives and had little, if any, criminal history.

The recently thwarted plot by homegrown jihadists, in May 2007, against Fort Dix in New Jersey, only underscores the seriousness of this emerging threat. Understanding this trend and the radicalization process in the West that drives "unremarkable" people to become terrorists is vital for developing effective counterstrategies.

Americans paid the price for the blindness of their federal watchdogs, both at Fort Hood (where military psychiatrist, Malik Nadal Hasan, claimed 43 lives at the military base in 2009) and in the case of the Tsarnaev brothers in Boston in 2013. On both occasions, there were clear signs or alerts indicating a risk situation, which were either ignored or underestimated.

Nowadays, the threat comes from hybrid and opportunist groups, capable of rapid transformation. There is a new criminal "melting pot" that includes religious fanaticism, massacres, piracy, human trafficking, drugs, weapons, toxic substances, and diamonds. A criminal-terrorist continuum or gangster-terrorism is emerging which no longer reflects neat office pigeonholes cleverly prepared for them by major intelligence agencies. Bureaucracies have failed to seize the complexity of the situation and are desperately trying to fit reality to their vision of it. Reality is rarely adaptable.

New terrorist profiles have emerged. The backbone is formed by radical Muslims who have corrupted their religion, and new converts, but there are also non-ideological groups like the Mafia gangs who, for example in the Sahel, have agreed to act as the "subcontractors" of terrorist groups while they pursue their usual trafficking activities.

Hundreds of young men between two cultures, born or raised in the West but unsure of their roots, leave their homes to fight in Afghanistan, Chechnya, Bosnia, or Syria in wars that they have not declared. They do so in the name of a cause, their faith, a fight they consider just. What label we attach to them (terrorist, resistance fighter, or combatant) is of no importance, the issue is how their return home and the potential danger that they present should be managed.

NOT SUCH LONE WOLVES

In the Merah case, the concept of the lone wolf terrorist was brandished by the security and intelligence services and journalists as an easy explanation following a failure. The French Interior Minister is the only person currently to have avoided this simplistic approach and escaped the prevailing trend. We should therefore look back at the origins of this term and explain why it very rarely reflects the reality of the situation.

The term seems to have been used first in the 1990s in the U.S., coined by Tom Metzger, founder of White Aryan Resistance (WAR), following on from being a leader of the Ku Klux Klan and a democratic candidate in congressional elections. After sizable damages were awarded against both him and his organization for racist crime, Tom Metzger set about promoting "lone wolf attacks" against the system.

Later, the FBI popularized the term by launching "Operation Lone Wolf" against San Diego white supremacists, formed into small independent cells.

The cornerstone of the term is an absence of specific orders or instructions. Lane wolves can share the same interests or the same "faith" but are not answerable to anybody. According to Ramon Spaaij "lone wolves are characterized by the fact that they act on their own, do not belong to any organized terrorist network or group and their modi operandi are conceived and carried out by the individual without external orders or hierarchy. They follow their own strong political, ideological or religious convictions, plan their actions with care and can successfully hide their operations from the people they frequent." Spaaij draws a distinction between lone wolves and "lone madmen" whose objective is "intrinsically idiosyncratic (*Larousse Dictionary*: way of being specific to each individual), completely egocentric and profoundly personal."

DISTANCE DOES NOT EQUATE TO INDEPENDENCE

Over the years, researchers have focused on finding a methodology for identifying autonomous but not independent cells and the individuals assuming total command over their actions. Ramon Spaaij, Raffaello Pantucci, Jeffrey Simon, and Jean Marc Flukiger have, rather successfully, tried their hands at coining a definition, which still seems to have some way to go.

Among the most coherent examples are total lone wolves, who possess their own expressed ideology, generally passed on in a reference work, who possess or build up their own weapons arsenal and take orders from no-one (Théodore Kaczynski, the so-called "Unabomber," active in the U.S. between 1976 and 1995, David

Copeland, a nail-bomb specialist operating in London in 1999, and Anders Breivik in Norway in 2011). To these individuals, we can add the assassins of public figures such as Robert Kennedy or Pim Fortuyn, who act according to motivations and modi operandi which can be said to include them in this group.

There are other cases, such as Khaled Khelkhal in France in 1995, Mohammed Merah in Toulouse in 2012, Timothy McVeigh (the Oklahoma City bomber in 1995), Franz Fuchs (who mailed 25 letter-bombs in Austria in the 1990s), Nidal Malik Hassan (the military psychiatrist who killed or injured 43 people in Fort Hood in 2009), Farouk Abdulmutallab (the underwear bomber on Flight NW 253 in 2009), Richard Reid (the shoe bomber on Flight AA63 at the end of 2001), where operatives acted in isolation but maintained strong relationships with organized groups involving regular direct or indirect contact with terrorist group leaders or preachers, leading us to classify them in the autonomous but not independent category.

This also appears to be the case of the Tsarnaev brothers (the recent Boston bombers) or Michael Adbolajo and Michael Adebonwale, known or reported to U.S and UK intelligence services, and many others improperly included in the lone wolf category. Some work in twos. This should logically influence the label we give them. Alas, this has little influence on established news pundits

In the case of Raffaello Pantucci, a "pack wolves" category might seem apt, affording us greater understanding but a link with organizations, however tenuous, significantly reduces the size of this category (a few cases: Milan, Cologne, or Fort Dix).

Shortsightedness in Routine Labeling

Investigations and commissions of enquiry have systematically found that almost all the relevant intelligence was already known before bombings occurred and that the Western ability never to hear what terrorists say, proclaim, and write is the key failing enabling them to commit their atrocities. In time, we may well find a better method of reclassification than the current routine labeling to make good the existing shortcomings.

There are also a small number of lone madmen, lone wolves, and autonomous operatives who are in a position to take action. In a few years, we have moved on from hyper-terrorism to gang-terrorism, and then to Lumpen-terrorism, with the vestiges of each phase surviving in a single territory or within a group more resilient than others. According to Spaaij, who, in an appendix to his book, lists 88 cases (between 1968 and 2010), the activists of all categories combined, correctly classified or not, would appear to represent less than 2% of recorded attacks in the Rand Corporation terrorism database. Although they may be less effective, less spectacular than the mass atrocities which bear the signature of what we feel obliged to call Al Qaeda, these «wasp stings» caused by micro attacks (that also marked the Maghreb and Israel, with the knife and bulldozer incidents) nevertheless cause disruption to everyday life, particularly if we allow every micro event, even the dramatic ones, the same media coverage as 9/11.

DEATH THROES

The present situation seems more marked by death throes (that can obviously be long-lasting) than by a new wave or new generation with greater focus on action in the field (after Chechnya, Kosovo, Libya, or in Syria, which seems to be replicating a modern version of the Spanish Civil War). In any event, the time has come for the authorities to leave behind the security of their bureaucratic categorizations and the pigeonholes into which they love placing criminals, based on purely clerical preordinations. We need to focus on these "hybrid" phenomena, at the heart of what is to come and not what has gone by.

AGE OF LUMPEN-TERRORISM

Karl Marx devised the concept of the "Lumpenproletariat" (a rag, dispossessed, or under proletariat) in his book *The German Ideology* of 1845. The emergence of "Lumpen Terrorists" is a matter of great concern. They stir up the same storm of media coverage as any terrorist attack with much more serious consequences but, above all, they seriously complicate early detection work. As an example, the murder of a British soldier in civilian clothing leaving his barracks in South London by two individuals armed with knives and a hatchet was a sad reminder of the knife or bulldozer attacks that punctuated the 1990s in Israel and the Maghreb.

Faced with increasing difficulties in planning major operations in the West, the shadowy Jihadists have resigned themselves to inciting solitary individuals, who are not lone wolves, to act with whatever means and resources are available to them.

Paradoxically, aside from the horror of their acts and the suffering of the victims and their loved-ones, this trend seems less a renewal than the final death spasms at the end of a cycle that began with the Declaration of War against Americans of 1996.

A new and different phase will undoubtedly begin, drawing vindication, as is often the case, from known and identified causes. Yet, we should never slacken our attention of the fundamentals, the tensions between Israel and Iran. The battlefield has been partially shifted to Syria. The choice between ever-more jihadist militants and an Alaouite State apparatus supported by Hezbollah does not make western government decision-making any easier. After the liberation of Libya, the post Arab Spring situations in Egypt and Tunisia encourage great caution. After all, as Henry Kissinger said when talking about the Iran-Iraq War, "it's a shame they both can't lose."

The subtle nature of the behaviors involved in radicalization makes identification or even surveillance difficult from a law application standpoint. Considered separately, various forms of conduct can be seen as harmless. However, once they are perceived as components in a radicalization process continuum, their significance becomes much more worrying. The sequence of these behaviors and the need to identify those who engage in the process at the earliest possible stage, make intelligence essential to thwarting a terrorist attack or preventing the planning of future atrocities.

Analyzing new threats requires an understanding of the real risks since the fall of the Berlin Wall. However, we also need to understand the operational logic of terror activists. Terrorist groups are not "organizations" as we might understand the term in the West. They do not have rigid or pyramid structures. They are fluid, liquid, volatile. They are not like the IRA or ETA. For a long time, my colleague Xavier Raufer and I have described and examined the nature of what we still feel inclined to call Al Qaida, with its nebular DNA, its collegial, decentralized and franchised working structure.

The radicalization process, boosted by the Internet, no longer requires adepts to attend a training camp. It is no longer necessary to be "chemically pure" to join the Jihad.

NOT FIGHTING THE WRONG WAR

Our detection, identification, and tracking tools are formatted by operators who firmly believe, sometimes too deeply, in their electronic hardware. ECHELON did not prevent 9/11, the Madrid, or London bombings, or dozens of later attempts pursued from virtually anywhere, particularly from within the boundaries of U.S. military installations at Fort Dix in 2007 or Fort Hood in 2009. PRISM did not stop the Boston attacks and was not able to identify the spy of spies, Edward Snowden, leaving him free to reveal State secrets to the entire planet. The system has come up short every time, because of a programming error, a mistake of perspective, or in control rather than in the quality of its operators or procedures.

Accepting what is different, evolving or changing, is at the heart of the process of detection and global security. It is not a matter of considering that all egg thieves are destined to become terrorists, but simply of not ruling out that some of them may do so on ideological or theological grounds, especially when there are more and more examples of more or less solitary auto-radicalization occurring around the world.

The fight against terrorism is not a war in the military sense but rather a matter of policing. It requires clear identification of the opponent. As in the medical field, we need to proceed in a logical order: diagnosis, prognosis, and treatment. Without the first step, there is fallibility in the others. Terrorism in its current form no longer resembles the terrorism of decades gone by. We are only surprised by what we do not wish to see, frequently confusing microscope and telescope or using them from the wrong end, seeing everything in a blur.

The master of criminologists, Sherlock Holmes, often said: "once you have eliminated the impossible, whatever remains, no matter how improbable, must be the truth." It is within our reach provided we decide simply to accept reality and its changes.

With the force and speed of a tsunami, the economy and finance are becoming digital. Ever faster, ever more stridently, the economy is becoming a cyber-economy, and finance, cyber-finance. Always and everywhere, criminals are predators. New spheres of predation open up and they rush headlong in, all the more so because they are bound by none of the honest world's constraints. They can move on, from one day to the next, from narcotics to trafficking in toxic waste, and from there on to cyber-crime. Let us look at what this new "adventure playground" has to offer villains, spies, and terrorists, and what is happening there.

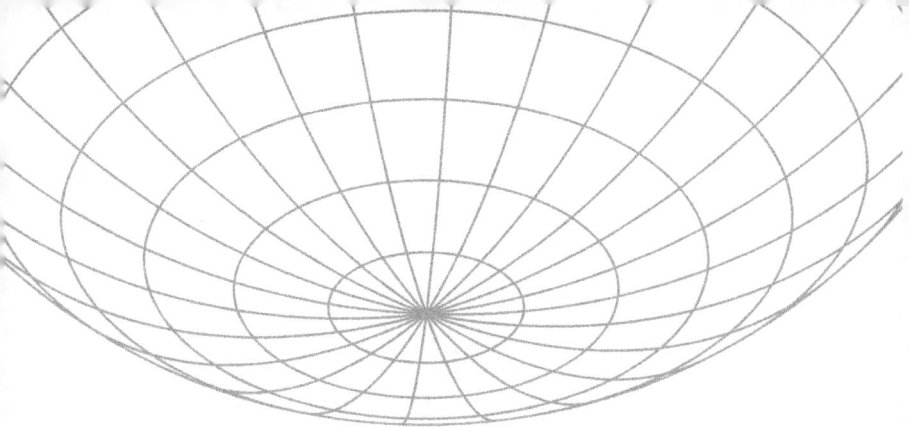

CRIME, WAR, TERRORISM, ESPIONAGE, AND SURVEILLANCE IN CYBERSPACE: BEYOND THE REIGNING CONFUSION

Not a day goes by without news of a successful hacking operation into public or private secure servers, the plundering of a bank ATM, an announcement that a hacker has seized control of a water or electricity network, medical or even surveillance devices... However, we rarely hear talk of what is vital, the heart of the network, its hidden reaches.

We pretend, every time, to be discovering the problem for the first time. ECHELON, CARNIVORE, and PRISM, more and more intrusive tools, but does anyone really know whether they live up to their claimed effectiveness in the fight against terrorism?

There has been no real echo of the apocalyptic predictions of the first years that we knew about the hacking process. Any real success of cyber-fraud campaigns has, in general, required the unwitting support of numerous victims interested in enlarging their reproductive organs, increasing their nighttime capabilities, or enjoying the windfall of recovering a few million dollars stolen by an illustrious stranger, suddenly deceased, whose widow calls for support via the Internet. However, more recent developments tend to suggest that a new plateau has been reached, in terms of the expansion of the number of accounts targeted by falsifying power company emails, for example, but also in terms of the technical means used, such as ransomware concealed behind a purported message from a public authority (IRS or Customs).

Money laundering using prepaid bank cards has also become a matter of concern, especially when considering the perverse effects of the market deregulation measures taken by the European Union.

DIGITAL DECOMPARTMENTALIZATION

Myriam Quemener, one of the rare judges to have given due thought to the extent of the problem, emphasized the difficulty in involving the judicial apparatus in the fight against cyber-crime because it is one of the rare areas that does not yet have a clearly defined criminal law policy. Also, the use of digital networks implies a decompartmentalization of the various forms of criminal activity and further confirms a trend towards criminal fusion and the hybridization of activities incorporating terrorism.

Criminals are at the same time hackers, protection racketeers, agents of influence or of States, and militants. These network mercenaries act in a "free exchange" area and on behalf of the highest bidder, yet, like the hackers' collective, Anonymous, still retain a true commitment to their claimed values. This situation partially explains the Wiki leaks that swept aside the principal U.S. programs, which are by far the most developed despite the galloping progress of the Chinese.

The problem lies in the general confusion in which criminal predation, espionage, server jamming, data blocking, or destruction are jumbled up despite there being specific logic behind each of these actions or tactics.

THE CRUX OF THE MATTER LIES ELSEWHERE

We rarely address the essential despite it being the heart of the network and its hidden parts that matter.

The most vital Internet components are the root servers.

The function of a root server is to respond to searches on top-level domain names and to redirect them towards the relevant top-level DNS servers (.com, .fr, .org, etc). There are currently 13 root servers in operation, identified by letters from "A" to "M." Ten of them are in the U.S., including «G» which belongs to the Department of Defense; "K" is in London, "I" in Stockholm, and "M" in Tokyo. There are none in France.

These ultra-protected servers are the constant targets of denial of service or "Ddos" attacks. Their purpose is to gridlock the network with hundreds of thousands (or even millions) of simultaneous searches. The servers are unable to cope with this level of demand and they are therefore quickly disabled. As the Internet has hundreds of millions of users, the consequences of a breakdown or the destruction of central points of the network could be catastrophic.

The principal threat comes from organizations motivated by ideological, political, or religious convictions whose target is the U.S. (as the authorities responsible for managing the servers). They build up arsenals of virtual weapons in readiness for attacking the Internet.

DIGITAL INDEPENDENCE

We may wonder why France still does not have its own root server so that it can protect its system and ensure that its smooth-running according to its own safety protocols so that it can continue using it in degraded mode operation if the U.S. systems should go offline (which is far from impossible considering that coordinated attacks against root servers have already been recorded, notably in 2002 and 2007). The objective is all the more important because server management has been entrusted to private organizations (other than the NASA and U.S. Defense servers). They consider security to be a confidential matter and share their security data with no-one. A country has no choice but to trust an entity over which it has absolutely no control despite the fact that it is custodian of the basis for all of its means of electronic communication, unless France has a guarantee of total control over its server within the U.S., as it does for its embassy, which seems highly unlikely (and this is clearly an understatement).

There have been notable and significant efforts on the part of the Russian, Chinese (and Iranian) authorities to equip themselves with more or less independent tools.

The second matter for concern relates to Internet Exchange Points. These are nerve centers affording access to the worldwide web, improving data traffic but using multiple routing configurations with a higher tolerance to breakdowns over the entire territory.

IXPs (Internet Exchange Points) or GIXs (Global Internet Exchanges) are physical infrastructures used by various Internet service providers (Free, Orange, Bouygues, SFR, etc.) to exchange traffic between their independent systems networks through their mutual "peering agreements." These exchanges allow for greater fluidity of traffic at a low cost, enabling millions of users based in regions where population is less dense than in major cities to use the Internet. The service providers are private entities and, like the U.S. organizations that manage the root servers, they decide individually on how their own security policy is applied (with all the risks that this entails). In addition to the various forms of electronic attack (Ddos, malicious code, polymorphic code, or malware, etc.), these organizations may fall victim to physical attacks (cable cutting, total or partial destruction of their operations centers, etc.).

The larger and more complex a network is, the more difficult it is to clean it after infection by a virus. Some national and foreign institutions still have painful memories of such infections, having spent months trying to rid themselves of a virus without certainty of their success.

Alain Bauer

A MAJOR THREAT

Espionage of the organizations managing communications is a major threat. Many State services
themselves admit that an increasing number of Trojan
horses are being installed and activated on networks
on which the traffic contains a considerable amount
of sensitive data. The real ability of service providers
to detect malicious code, introduced with the aim of
recovering confidential or strategic information rather
than damaging or undermining a network, seems very
feeble especially when they are the coerced or voluntary
accomplices of such operations. It is difficult, under the
guise of fighting terrorism, to resist the temptation of
eavesdropping on the communications of competing
businesses in an international tendering procedure or
gathering information from major industrial concerns
or research centers, etc.

The other critical component is to do with the
underside or invisible portion of the Internet that
represents more than 70% of its overall space and
contains 500 times more data in an area unreachable
by conventional search tools. This Dark Internet (or
Deep Web) which, like the visible web, uses tools developed by the military (e.g. the TOR network invented
by the U.S. Navy) to encrypt and depersonalize web
access, provides a means for managing very large num-
bers of connections, whatever their source, without
any form of viable control or oversight, including of
those attempting to defend rights and freedoms and
traffickers of all denominations.

It is clear from network and tool expansion and high interconnection and linkup growth that the cyber-risk is unlikely to disappear. The Cloud, like its climatic namesake, could be quickly carried away by a storm, thunder, and lightning.

We know that the "Latest Crime News" will certainly not be the last, just the most recent and often the most inadequately covered. As always, but more than ever, the crime world is showing an adaptive genius and innovation. It is now down to crime prevention professionals to prove themselves just as creative as the underworld, knowing that if they cannot anticipate, they must at least achieve early detection of the many demons dwelling on the dark side of globalization.

ABOUT ALAIN BAUER

Professor, Chair of criminology, National Conservatory of Arts and Crafts CNAM (since 2009),

President of the National Private Security Control Council (CNAPS) (since 2012),

Co-President of the Mission for the White Book on Public Security (2010-2011),

President of the Strategic Research High Council to the President (since december 2009),

President of the Working Group on Customs Files (2009-2010),

President of the French National Crime Commission (2003-2013),

President of the Strategic Security Mission to the President (2007-2010),

President of the National CCTV Commission (2007-2011),

President of the Police Files Control Group (2006-2008),

Vice President of Francopol since 2009,

Member of the Honorary Committee of the International League Against Racism and Antisemitism (since 2003),

Former member of the High Authority against Discrimination (2005/2007),

Former member of the National Commission for Human Rights (2000/2003),

Former Advisor to the Prime Minister (Michel Rocard 1988/1990),

Former Vice President of the Sorbonne University (Paris I – 1981/1988),

Founding Member of SOS Racism (1985),

Visiting professor at the Sorbonne University (Paris I, Paris II, Paris V), at the Gendarmerie High Studies Center, at the National Magistrate's Academy, at the National Superior Police Academy,

Senior Fellow at the Terrorist Center of John Jay College of Criminal Justice in New York (USA), Senior Fellow at the Law and Political Science University of Beijing (PRC), at the Canadian Police College, at the Chinese Criminal Police Academy (Shenyang, PRC)....Member of the ICT International Advisory Board,

Auditor of the Ihesi,

Consultant for the New York Police Department (USA), the Los Angeles Sheriff Department (USA), the Sûreté du Québec (Canada),

Colonel of the Air Force (Reserve).

CRIMINOLOGICAL AND STRATEGIC BOOKS

Violences et insécurité urbaines (PUF 1998, 12ème éd. 2010),

L'Amérique, la violence, le crime (PUF 2000, 2ème éd. 2001),

La guerre ne fait que commencer (Jean-Claude Lattès 2002, Folio Gallimard 2003),

Les polices en France (PUF 2001, 3ème éd. 2010),

Le crime aux États-Unis (PUF 2003),

Les polices aux États-Unis (PUF 2003),

Dico Rebelle (Michalon 2004),

Imaginer la sécurité globale (La pensée et les hommes Bruxelles 2004),

État d'urgence (Robert Laffont 2004),

L'énigme Al Qaida (Jean Claude Lattès 2005),

Géographie criminelle de la France (Odile Jabob 2006),

World Chaos (DRMCC 2007),

Mieux contrôler les fichiers de police et de gendarmerie (Documentation Française 2007),

Radicalization in the West (NYPD 2007),

Vers une plus grande efficacité du service public de sécurité au quotidien (Documentation Française 2007),

Le nouveau chaos mondial (Les riaux 2007),

La criminalité en France (CNRS Editions 2007),

Déceler, étudier, former : une voie nouvelle pour la recherche stratégique (INHES 2008),

Jeux en ligne et menaces criminelles (Rapport au ministre des comptes, 2008),

Le 11 Septembre (Editions Ouest France 2008),

Année stratégique 2008,

Vidéosurveillance et vidéoprotection (PUF 2008),

Année stratégique 2009 (Dalloz 2008),

Terrorism Early Warning (LASD 2008),

La criminalité en France (CNRS Editions 2008),

Football et société (FFF 2008),

Sécurité privée en Europe (INHES 2008),

Criminologie Française (2009),

Les 100 mots de la police et du crime (PUF 2009),

Les fichiers de police et de gendarmerie (PUF 2009),

Les études de sécurité publique (PUF 2009),

La face noire de la mondialisation (CNRS Editions 2009),

Année stratégique 2010 (Dalloz 2009),

La criminalité en France (CNRS Editions 2009),

Le sens de la Liberté (PUL 2010),

Les terroristes écrivent toujours ce qu'ils vont faire (PUF 2010),

À la recherche de la criminologie (CNRS Editions 2010),

Année stratégique 2011 (Dalloz 2010),

Les 100 mots du terrorisme (PUF 2010),

Transnational criminology manual (Wolf Legal 2010),

Introduction générale à la criminologie (PUF 2010),

Statistiques criminelles et victimation (PUF 2010),

Les politiques publiques de sécurité (PUF 2011),

Violences et société aujourd'hui (ESH 2011),

Histoire criminelle de la France (Odile Jacob 2012),

La criminologie pour les nuls (First 2012). Dernieres nouvelles du criome (CNRS Editions 2013), Dictionnaire amoureux du crime (PLON 2012),

Histoire de l'anthropologie criminelle et de la médecine légale (PUF 2013).

BOOKS FOREWORDS

Insécurité : nouveaux risques (L'Harmattan 1998),

Entreprises, les 13 pièges du chaos mondial (PUF 2002),

Le flic et le thérapeute (Entrelacs 2005),

1000 jours pour vaincre l'insécurité (Creaphis 2005),

La France dans la guerre de l'information (L'harmattan 2006),

Pour une stratégie globale de sécurité nationale (Dalloz 2008),

L'Eau : Géopolitique, enjeux et stratégies (CNRS Editions 2008),

Guide de la sécurité au quotidien (Archipel 2008),

Les armes non létales (PUF 2009),

La Cyberguerre (Vuibert 2009),

La métamorphose du pouvoir (Vuibert 2009),

Le marché international du faux (CNRS Editions 2010),

L'État, la peur et le citoyen (Vuibert 2010),

Le renseignement criminel (CNRS Editions 2011),

Eau et conflictualités (Choiseul 2011),

L'insécurité, un scandale français (L'Œuvre 2012).

BOOKS SUPERVISION

Les polices au Québec (PUF 2006, 2ème édition 2006),

ADN et enquêtes criminelles (PUF 2008),

Les écoutes téléphoniques (PUF 2009)

Le renseignement par internet (PUF 2010),

La cybersécurité (PUF),

La guerre économique (PUF),

La sécurité privée en France (PUF).

TO BE PUBLISHED

Biométrie et identité (PUF),

La gestion de crise (PUF).

FEATURE ARTICLES

Le Syndicalisme étudiant, (Pouvoirs 26, 1983),

La Police, (Pouvoirs 102),

Sécurité, Crime, Entreprise, (Revue de Défense Nationale, Mars 2005 supplément),

La Criminalité Française, (Risques 51),

Repenser le débat sur l'insécurité, (Lettre du Cadre Territorial, HS1),

Les nouvelles problématiques de l'insécurité, (Maires de France, Octobre 2001),

Délinquance et violence aux États-Unis, (L'Histoire 242),

Insécurité et Statistiques, (Tribune du Commissaire de Police, 76),

Le Contrat Local de Sécurité, (Face au risque 353),

Sur mesure et sécurité, (Le Monde de l'Éducation 274),

Que fait la police ?, (Le Nouvel Observateur, 17 Février 2000),

Voyage à l'intérieur de la Police, (L'Histoire 240),

Ou sont les policiers ?, (La gazette des communes, 8 Février 1999),

Malveillance et sécurité publique, (Face au risque 340),

Violences urbaines, (Risques 38),

Grands équipements urbains et sécurité, (Lettre de l'IHESI 2),

La sécurité des Jeux Olympiques, (Cahiers de la Sécurité Intérieure 26),

Sécurité nationale (RDN 2007),

Une vocation nouvelle pour la criminologie (Sécurité Globale 2008),

Surprise, désordre et stratégie (RDN 2008),

Traçabilité et réseaux (Hermés 53),

La pensée stratégique (RDN 2009),

Le crime organisé, (Pouvoirs 132),

Les moyens de la fin, (Agir 40 2009),

Repenser l'éthique de la sécurité, (Sécurité et stratégie HS Septembre 2010),

Ultra Gauche (Sécurité Globale 12, Septembre 2010),

Outils stratégiques, (Revue de lka Défense Nationale 735, Décembre 2010),

Le monde criminel en 2030, (Revue Internationale et Stratégique 80, Décembre 2010),

Victimation des personnes âgées, (Administration Avril 2011),

Le monde face au vide de la pensée stratégique, (La Tribune, Juin 2011),

L'aube inquiétante du siècle ,(Sécurité Globale 16, Septembre 2011),

Géopolitique du crime, (Nouvelle revue de géopolitique, Octobre 2011),

Les émeutes urbaines de 2011 en Grande Bretagne, (ENA Magazine, Décembre 2011).

FILM SCENARIO

Rituels Meurtriers (France 2, Octobre 2011 & DVD Janvier 2012).

DISTINCTIONS

Captain of the Legion of Honor, of the National Order of Merit,

Commander of the National Order of Academic Palms and of the National Order of Arts and Letters.

Golden Rings of the International Olympic Commitee,

Grand Cross of the Lafayette Order, Medal of Honor of the National Police,

Medal of Honor of the National Gendarmerie,

Golden Oak of the Surete du Quebec,

Commandeur de l'Ordre du Mérite de la République Italienne.

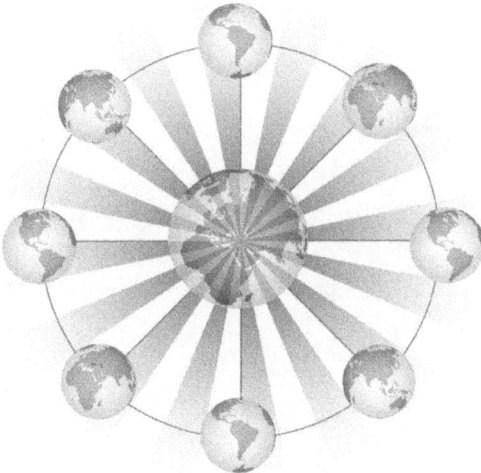

www.ingramcontent.com/pod-product-compliance
Lightning Source LLC
Chambersburg PA
CBHW032121280326
41933CB00009B/932